London

London

Terry Sackett

Waterton Press Limited

First published in the United Kingdom in 1998 by
Frith Publishing an imprint of Waterton Press Limited.

Text and Design Copyright © Waterton Press Limited

Photographs Copyright © The Francis Frith Collection.

British Library Cataloguing in Publication Data.

Terry Sackett
London

ISBN 1-84125-026-0

Typeset in Bembo Semi Bold

Printed and bound in Great Britain by
WBC Limited, Bridgend, Glamorgan.

Contents

Francis Frith 1822–1898

Francis Frith
A Victorian Pioneer

Francis Frith, the founder of the world famous photographic archive was a complex and multitudinous man. A devout Quaker and a highly successful and respected Victorian businessman he was also a flamboyant character.

By 1855 Frith had already established a wholesale grocery business in Liverpool and sold it for the astonishing sum of £200,000, equivalent of over £15,000,000 today. Now a multimillionaire he was able to indulge in his irresistible desire to travel. As a child he had poured over books penned by early explorers, and his imagination had been stirred by family holidays to the sublime mountain regions of Wales and Scotland. "What a land of spirit-stirring and enriching scenes and places!" he had written. He was to return to these scenes of grandeur in later years to "recapture the thousands of vivid and tender memories", but with a very different purpose. Now in his thirties, and captivated by the new science of photography, Frith set out on a series of pioneering journeys to the Middle East, that occupied him from 1856 until 1860.

He took with him a specially-designed wicker carriage which acted as camera, dark-room and sleeping chamber. These far-flung journeys were full of intrigue and adventure. In his life story, written when he was sixty-three, Frith tells of being held captive by bandits, and fighting "an awful midnight battle to the very point of exhaustion and surrender with a deadly pack of hungry, wild dogs. He bargained for several weeks with a "mysterious priest" over a beautiful seven-volume illuminated Koran, which is now in the British Museum. Wearing full arab costume, Frith arrived at Akaba by camel seventy years before Lawrence of Arabia, where he encountered "desert princes and rival sheikhs, blazing with jewel-hilted swords".

During these extraordinary adventures he was assiduously exploring the desert regions of the Nile and recording the antiquities and people with his camera, Frith was the first photographer ever to travel beyond the sixth cataract. Africa, we must remember, was still the "Dark Continent", and Stanley and Livingstone's famous meeting was a decade into the future. The conditions for picture taking confound belief. He laboured for hours on end in his dark-room in the sweltering heat, while the volatile collodion chemicals fizzed dangerously in their trays. Often he was forced to work in tombs and caves where conditions were cooler.
Back in London he exhibited his photographs and was "rapturously cheered" by the Royal Society. His reputation as a photographer was made overnight. His photographs were issued

in albums by James S. Virtue and William MacKenzie, and published simultaneously in London and New York. An eminent historian has likened their impact on the population of the time to that on our own generation of the first photographs taken on the surface of the moon.

Characteristically, Frith spotted the potential to create a new business as a specialist publisher of photographs. In 1860 he married Mary Ann Rosling and set out to photograph every city, town and village in Britain. For the next thirty years Frith travelled the country by train and by pony and trap, producing photographs that were keenly bought by the millions of Victorians who, because of the burgeoning rail network, were beginning to enjoy holidays and day trips to Britain's seaside resorts and beauty spots.

To meet the demand he gathered together a team of up to twelve photographers, and also published the work of independent artist-photographers of the reputation of Roger Fenton and Francis Bedford. Together with clerks and photographic printers he employed a substantial staff at his Reigate studios. To gain an understanding of the scale of Frith's business one only has to look at the catalogue issued by Frith & Co. in 1886. It runs to some 670 pages listing not only many thousands of views of the British Isles but also photographs of most major European countries, and China, Japan , the USA and Canada. By 1890 Frith had created the greatest specialist photographic publishing company in the world.

He died in 1898 at his villa in Cannes, his great project still growing. His sons, Eustace and Cyril, took over the task, and Frith & Co. continued in business for another seventy years, until by 1970 the archive contained over a third of a million pictures of 7,000 cities, towns and villages.

The photographic record he has left to us stands as a living monument to a remarkable and very special man.

Frith's dhow in Egypt c.1857

LONDON

Until the end of the eighteenth century London was a compact city. Its merchants lived in the square mile and the aristocracy in the more fashionable areas of Piccadilly and the West End. Beyond Park Lane, however, there was a wilderness of forest and mire, where footpads and highwayman lurked. Londoners were regularly accosted in the Strand. Many preferred to travel by water on the River Thames.

In the Victorian era the city grew at an extraordinary rate as the Empire spread and wealth returned to the coffers of the London banks. Whole neighbourhoods of ramshackle housing were demolished and the great thoroughfares we know today were created. Nash remodelled much of the West End, and great houses and mansions lined the leafy thoroughfares that were once grazing land for the city's flocks of sheep. Public spaces such as Trafalgar Square and Piccadilly Circus were created and richly embellished by public sculpture and memorials commemorating Britain's historic past.

The 1851 Great Exhibition symbolised the country's new wealth and prestige. The great glass halls conceived by Paxton were filled to bursting with triumphs of industry and engineering endeavour, and the world flocked to enjoy a glimpse of the exciting future.

The City of London developed gradually into the centre of world finance. London's burgeoning banks and insurance companies clamoured for space in the overcrowded square mile. Further widespread demolition followed, and new streets of Victorian Gothic offices were constructed, heavy and sepulchral in character. Here many thousands of clerks and office workers laboured day in and day out. Traffic congested the newly built or refurbished roads and bridges, and Londoners struggled with the complexities of city life very much as we do today.

The poor were ever present. Thousands of country people flocked to London with the promise of work. Yet with increasing mechanisation of production, traditional crafts and trades were swiftly superseded, throwing thousands into the streets to earn a few shillings. London's street traders were a legend, their guile and cunning offering them the only hope of survival in a hostile city.

For centuries London's wealth had been fuelled by river traffic. Great ships plied the estuary of the Thames to unload at the many new docks that were constructed as far upriver as London Bridge. The wharves and quays resounded with the cries of stevedores and dock workers unloading coal, timber and the raw materials of engineering. There were also exotic imports from China and Asia to tempt the wealthy.

By the time of Queen Victoria's Jubilee in 1897 the face of the capital would have been almost unrecognisable to an eighteenth century Londoner. The streets and buildings stretched out into the countryside and millions of people had moved out of the expensive centre to newly-built suburbs to become commuters. The rate of change had been bewildering and relentless. Everyone was touched by it and many suffered as a result of it. Yet there was no going back. London's expansion has never slowed since. With its beautiful streets and buildings, and its unique position as financial centre of Europe and the colonies, it had justly earned its reputation as the greatest city in the world.

L130084   Cheyne Walk, *c.*1890. This tranquil street of handsome houses fringing the river was built in 1708. Chelsea had long been the haunt of artists and writers - Thomas Carlyle lived at 5, Cheyne Walk for almost half a century. Other illustrious residents, including Philip Wilson Steer, Whistler and Rossetti, were his close neighbours. Boats squat in the mud under the embankment.

L130087   Cheyne Walk, 1890. A carriage with top-hatted coachman waits patiently outside one of Cheyne Walk's many grand Georgian brick houses. Graceful plane trees screen residents from the more boisterous life on the water. A fleet of barges, their sales furled, are berthed at the quay.

ALONG THE RIVER

Today the Thames is a little more than an obstacle for Londoners to cross. Commuters funnel over its old bridges towards the railway stations and suburbs. The river slides by below the parapets keeping its own counsel.

In Victorian times the river was the vital lifeline of the city, thronged with ships. Vessels sailed and steamed down the estuary to offload their cargoes at bustling docks all the way down to London Bridge. The quays were noisy with the cries of stevedores and labourers shifting coals and every manner of import and export. Smaller craft plied upriver, carrying produce to Thames-side towns and into the canals that threaded their way through the Midlands to the north.

With the coming of the railways and the motor vehicle the Thames entered a period of gradual and painful decline. Now it is almost the exclusive province of tourists who enjoy the vistas of the City from its breezy waters.

L130129   Albert Bridge, *c.*1900. Until 1878 all but three of the bridges over the Thames were owned by private companies who levelled tolls on foot passengers. In 1879 this beautiful bridge of three airy spans, topped with decorative towers, was made free for public access.

L130083   Chelsea Embankment, 1890. The Thames Embankment, which skirts the front of Cheyne Walk, was created by Sir Joseph Bazalgette. Constructed over mud flats, it conceals the sewers that were once a scourge of the locality. The barge in the photograph, its sail furled, is loaded with straw. These old vessels were vital carriers of coal, fruit, vegetables and building materials from Kent, Essex and other east-coast ports.

L130120   Lambeth Riverside, 1880. This Lambeth river frontage presents a very different face to the more refined Chelsea scene across the river. Here is a clutter of ramshackle warehouses, timber-yards and wharves. The flimsy houses were clearly not designed to face the water, for the windows are few and diminutive. The crumbling façades bring a clear impression of neglect and poverty.

L130303   Westminster Bridge, *c.*1900. This fine bridge is one of the most dazzling structures spanning London's river and was constructed in 1862 at the cost of £250,000. With the waters at low tide as they are here, critics have suggested the bridge has an ungraceful 'lanky' appearance. Its uniquely light construction was the cause of trepidation amongst Londoners, for passengers on horse- drawn buses felt a distinct and unnerving vibration under the wheels as they passed over.

L130189 Victoria Embankment, 1890. A steamer, with a party of sightseers on board, has just left the quay heading down river. The women cluster at the stern under parasols. A little further along on the left is Cleopatra's Needle. This far-famed monument was transported to Britain through the treacherous Bay of Biscay from the deserts of Egypt, where it had lain buried and forgotten in the sands. It took considerable ingenuity to erect it in such a close space, for it is almost seventy ft in height.

L130052 Old Waterloo Bridge, 1895. Gulls forage for food in the frozen wastes. The ice has broken and the waters of the river released. Canova considered the old Waterloo Bridge, with its nine elliptical arches, to be one of the most magnificent in Europe. Originally called Strand Bridge, it was opened in 1817 on the anniversary of the Battle of Waterloo.

L130155 Old Waterloo Bridge, 1902. This panorama of the river through broad lawns and lofty trees reveals the bridge's graceful character. Engineered by John Rennie, it was well over 1,000 feet long and surmounted by an open balustrade. In 1924, after engineering reports of a dangerous weakening of one of the main arches, the old bridge was closed to traffic. Work on the new Waterloo Bridge was started in 1937.

L130077 Embankment from Temple Pier, 1890. The delightful Temple Gardens once extended right the way down to the river. Here were clipped green lawns and exquisite quadrangles. The fortunate few could enjoy a few precious moments away from the bustle of the city streets above. The imposing arch is in the monumental Egyptian style. In the background is Waterloo Bridge.

L130070 **Blackfriars Bridge, 1890.** The halfpenny toll on the original Blackfriars Bridge caused riots, and in 1780 angry protesters burned down the toll-house. After a succession of expensive repairs a replacement was suggested, and the present bridge was erected in 1864 at a cost of £265,000. With its colossal piers, and recesses set on short pillars of polished Aberdeen granite, Blackfriars Bridge has been censured by critics for being 'gaudy'. Rising over it is a magnificent prospect of St Paul's Cathedral.

L130017 Waterfront by St Paul's, 1890. This famous vista, taken from Bankside, shows the glorious dome of St Paul's rising over the roofs of London. The river is edged not with the anonymous and monumental office blocks we see today but with a pleasing clutter of wharves and warehouses. The river was a populous place of work where Thames barges and a thousand other vessels plied. On the right is the colliery wharf of the Weardale Iron and Coal Company.

L130034 London Bridge, 1890. The traffic jam is clearly not a modern phenomenon. London Bridge is thronged with cabs, carriers, brewers' drays, hay wagons, omnibuses and carriages. A dense procession of top-hatted gentlemen hurry along the pavement to their city offices. London Bridge's lamp-posts were cast from the metal of French cannons captured in the Peninsula War.

L130178   London Bridge, c.1890. So busy was London bridge at peak times that the authorities were compelled to station police constables along the central rib of the roadway to encourage a smooth flow of traffic. All vehicles moving at walking pace were ushered abruptly to the kerb sides so that swifter carriages could enjoy a clear passage.

L130317   London Bridge, c.1900. This five-arched granite structure was constructed in 1827 from the designs of John Rennie. Its excessive cost was once the talk of the city. Estimates ran as high as two and a half million pounds. In 1869 it was faced with cubes of Aberdeen granite. In the background is the imposing column of the Monument.

L1330019 Opening of Tower Bridge, 1894. The bridge was formally opened with great pomp and ceremony on 30 June 1894. The flags are flying on the steamers, one of which is being hauled along by a tugboat. These pleasure crafts are packed to the gunwhales with dignitaries celebrating the great event.

L130519   Tower Bridge, *c.*1890. The raised footway at the top of the towers, 140 ft above the level of the river, was closed in 1909 after a spate of suicides. In the foreground lies the Pool of London, the province of London watermen for generations. The river, at the end of Victoria's reign, is still busy with flat barges and sailing ships. In the background are the pinnacles of the Tower of London.

L130046   Tower Bridge, 1895. A steam tugboat hauls a barge into the docks on the right. St. Katharine's Dock was built in 1828. Some of the dock developments were massive in scale, revealing the scale of shipping using the Thames. The West India Docks on the Isle of Dogs could receive up to six hundred ships.

L130056 Thames Shipbuilding, *c*.1910. It is dawn and stevedores, carpenters, coopers and ropemakers are arriving by boat to begin the day's toil. They clamber eagerly up the rickety steps to stake their claim to work - most were poorly-paid casual workers hired daily. The thicket of wooden scaffolds would give a modern-day health and safety inspector a heart attack.

L130057   Thames Wharf, 1910. Henry Mayhew describes a typical dockside scene: 'The cooper is hammering at the casts on the quay; the chains of the cranes, loosed of their weight, rattle as they fly up; the ropes splash in the water; some captain shouts his orders . . .' London's river had been the source of its prosperity for centuries. However, by 1910 the industry was parlously overmanned, and the docks had gone into sharp decline. In 1888 the East and West India Company had been forced into bankruptcy.

L130058

Tower Bridge, 1910. Where London's other bridges are dignified and utilitarian, Tower Bridge, with its 'daring majesty' cocks a snook at Victorian formality. Barry permitted Sir Horace Jones to encase his steel skeleton in stone until it resembled an iced cake. Mock Gothic turrets were added, a profusion of sharply arched windows and much other sham detailing. To many, the stupendous structure had the look of an ornate medieval castle.

L130061 Tower Bridge Opening, c.1895. Uniquely for London bridges, the bascules of Tower Bridge can be raised or lowered to permit the passage of high-peaked vessels. Driven by steam, the hydraulic machinery hoisted the heavy 1,000 ton bascules to their raised positions in two minutes.

L130185 A Thames Wharfside View, *c.*1886. In this ramshackle scene, flat-bottomed coal barges squat in the mud alongside a collier's wharf. By 1850 much of the coal hauled to London from the Northern coalfields was offloaded by steam power. Yet upriver, above London Bridge, were the more modest colliers, whose simple barges, loaded by man-power, carried consignments on to Thameside towns, for shipment to the Midlands and the north through the canal network.

THE WEST END

The West End has long been the most fashionable region of London. Simply having an address there was an advantage. Robert Southey said that his tailor lived at the West End of Town, 'and consequently he is supposed to make my coat in a better style of fashion'.

The West End streets were designed and created by Britain's most celebrated architects, men of calibre and vision, such as Wren, Nash and Inigo Jones. The magnificent thoroughfares like the Strand, Piccadilly and Regent Street are world-renowned, and the great and the good promenaded their pavements savouring the delights of fashionable hotels, restaurants and art galleries. The mansions of Mayfair and the clubs of Pall Mall were the places to impress and be impressed. Broad, leafy squares offered the wealthy peace and tranquillity in the very midst of the 'monstrous city'. Great public spaces like Trafalgar Square, Piccadilly and the parks drew crowds of Londoners for civic events and occasions. They cheered and roared their approval as royalty processed in stately fashion from their palaces into the public streets.

The West End was created out of the profits of aristocratic capitalism. It enjoyed a unique flavour, and no other region of London has ever managed to compete with it.

L130086   Cheyne Walk, 1890. Away from the boisterous life of the river, Cheyne Walk, with its narrow, balconied houses and modish shops, was a haven of gentility, dedicated to refined if somewhat Bohemian pursuits. In the background is Chelsea Old Church, a fourteenth century building with a later steeple. It suffered extensive bomb damage in the War.

L130123 Waterman's Arms, Chelsea, 1875. In narrow alleys leading down to the river, similar to the one depicted here, there was an abundance of small taverns and public houses catering for the working man. Bargemen from the fleets that tied up below came here after the day's toil for conversation and community.

L130171 Rotten Row, 1890. Hyde Park has been called London's park 'par excellence'. Rotten Row, a corruption of route du roi, was a ride set aside for equestrians and fashionable promenaders. During afternoons in the London season, it was densely thronged with carriages parading their smart passengers around at little more than walking pace. The inevitable more refined traffic jams ended in polite deadlock.

L130166 Park Lane, 1890. Park Lane, once the desolate by-road known as Tiburn Lane, was a refined street of palatial mansions enjoying expansive vistas of the Park. These great houses included Grosvenor House, the home of the Marquess of Westminster, Holdernesse House, the residence of the Marquess of Londonderry, and Dorchester House.

L130035 Park Lane, 1900. This graceful ornamental fountain was erected in 1875 at the southern end of Park Lane at the junction with Hamilton Place. Designed by Sir Hamo Thornycroft, it incorporates three heroic-size marble figures of Shakespeare, Milton and Chaucer. The statue is surmounted by the gilded bronze winged figure of Fame, poised with one foot on a globe.

L130105 Hyde Park, 1890. Hyde Park extends from Piccadilly westwards to Kensington Gardens. Its 360 acres of open green space were called by William Pitt 'the lung of London'. 'Here', writes Thomas Miller, 'the pride and beauty of England may be seen upon their own stage; and on a fine day in the season no other spot in the world can outrival in rich display and chaste grandeur the scene which is here presented'.

L130169   Hyde Park Corner, 1900. Only a century and a half ago Hyde Park was bordered by mire and wilderness. Londoners tended market gardens close by which are now smothered by the buildings of Kensington. In the eighteenth century it was considered foolhardy to venture here after dark. Travellers joined forces to ward off the attentions of highwaymen.

L130202   The Wellington Arch, Hyde Park Corner, 1915. The arch of this impressive monument was originally crowned by Wyatt's colossal equestrian statue of the England's military darling, the Iron Duke. In the 1880s, when the French wars were long forgotten, it was moved to Aldershot and replaced by the dramatic bronze by Adrian Jones, an allegorical rendering of Peace dropping out of the heavens onto the chariot of war.

L130151   Hyde Park Corner, *c.*1908. The handsome triple-arched gateway, with its classical screen and groups of Ionic columns, was intended originally to create a noble approach to the Park from Buckingham Palace. It was designed and built in 1828 by Decimus Burton. The omnibus on the right, heading for Pimlico, is advertising the famous furnishing and decorating emporium of Maples.

L130003   Hyde Park Corner, 1910. Decimus Burton's impressive arch is topped by a decorative frieze depicting horsemen, the design imitated from the Elgin Marbles which were on display in the British Museum. So much of this luxurious neighbourhood mimics the glories of classical Greece.

L130238   Apsley House, Piccadilly, c.1920. To the right of the arch is Apsley House, one of only two or three of Piccadilly's great houses to survive. Known popularly as 'Number One, London', it was built by Robert Adam in the 1770s. It was bought by the Duke of Wellington in 1817 and here were held the glittering banquets celebrating the victory at Waterloo until his death in 1852.

L130173   Buckingham Palace, c.1890. In the time of James I the leafy grounds where this celebrated royal palace now stands grew mulberry bushes for the silk industry. The palace was built in its original form in the early 1700s and adapted to the Palladian style by John Nash in the 1830s. The Lord Chamberlain was always inundated with requests to view from the public, but permits were only granted to view the royal stables.

L1305050 Buckingham Palace and The Mall, *c.*1955. Marble Arch stood here in the Mall until 1850, when it was removed to its present position at the top of Park Lane. The Mall, an expansive and formal approach to the Palace, is fringed with limes, planes and elms, and skirts the north side of the diminutive St James's Park. Here, in freezing winters, Londoners enjoyed skating on the pond.

L130051   Piccadilly, 1910. This illustrious thoroughfare was once one of the two main routes leading westwards out of London. Because of its proximity to open parkland the wealthy clamoured to move here. From the eighteenth century onwards houses, mansions and shops were built that were to bring the street its reputation for refined living. In Piccadilly are the stylish Burlington and Piccadilly Arcades, the Ritz, and the Royal Academy.

L130002   Piccadilly Circus, 1890. This famous junction of crossways was once known as Regent Circus and developed out of Nash's elegant modelling of Regent Street. George IV likened Piccadilly Circus to an illusion of preventing 'the sensation of crossing Piccadilly being perceived'. In 1886 many of its buildings were demolished and the open space considerably enlarged.

L130036   Piccadilly Circus, *c.*1890. Dominating this view is the classical portico of the London Pavilion, one wing of which was occupied by the Piccadilly Restaurant. Here the well-heeled flocked to dine. It is hard to believe that this elegant corner of the West End is now smothered with giant neon advertisements. Opposite is the Criterion Restaurant, 'in whose spacious saloons one may rub shoulders with the representatives of every civilised nation'.

L130186   Eros and Piccadilly Circus, 1887. The glittering fountain depicting Eros was a memorial to the philanthropic nobleman Lord Shaftesbury. He died in 1886 and this photograph shows the fountain soon after it was erected. It was designed by Sir Alfred Gilbert, and when challenged about its impropriety at the time, supporters pointed out that it was 'purely symbolical and illustrative of Christian charity'.

L130038   Piccadilly Circus, *c.*1890. The city's horse-drawn omnibuses were operated by the London General Company. This Brixton Church to Charing Cross service was identified by its green coachwork. To tread the stage of the London Pavilion, shown behind, was the loftiest ambition of the music hall artiste. The Piccadilly Restaurant has been taken over by the Spaten Beer Company.

L130002   Piccadilly Circus, *c.*1910. Loafers of all kinds sit on the steps under Eros. The tradition for oversized hoardings and signboards has already been set. Mellin's Foods and Perrier Water shout their sales messages across the expansive space.

L130163 Regent Street and The Quadrant, 1900. Conceived and built by John Nash in 1813, this famous thoroughfare has been said to represent 'the highest beauty of street architecture.' The bold, sweeping curve of the Quadrant originally incorporated an open Doric arcade of 270 columns supporting a balustraded roof. However, the heavy cast shadows attracted 'undesirable company' and the arcade was eventually removed in 1848.

L130079 Regent Street, c.1890. This view looks north towards Oxford Street. Nash's handsome terraces were spurned by London's affluent classes, for stucco was considered common. Some said that his glorious creation was compromised by poor building work, but all agreed that Nash conjured for this region of the West End a genteel and polished atmosphere that has considerably added to its prosperity down the years.

L130206   Regent Circus, 1890. This central section of Regent Street follows the line of the old Swallow Street, where London's notorious highwaymen left their horses in livery. The street rigidly defined the neighbourhoods of rich and poor. To the west were the magnificent homes of society families and to the east a poor and wretched neighbourhood, part of which became Soho. In the foreground is a Hurdy Gurdy man.

L130225   Regent Street, 1900. A contemporary guidebook suggests that in Regent Street were to be found 'pedestrians of every class, from the fashionable lounger to the street Arab; from the duchess to the work-girl; . . . the bewigged and padded roué . . . ; from the quietly-dressed English gentleman to the flashily-arrayed foreign count of doubtful antecedents'.

L1350054 The National Gallery from Duncannon Street, 1897. The paintings that formed the basis of Britain's national collection were purchased for £57,000 in 1824 from J. Angerstein. The exhibition halls created on the north side of Trafalgar Square to display the lavish canvases were not universally admired. One Victorian critic believed 'the authorities showed a frugal mind in the low elevation of the building with its pepper-box turrets and insignificant dome'. The Corinthian pillars were rescued from Carlton House.

L130133   St Martin-in-the-Fields Church, Trafalgar Square, 1890. This exquisite Royal church was designed and erected by the architect James Gibbs in the 1720s. The expansive portico is generally admired, but the heavy steeple is said to lack elegance. Nell Gwynne was buried here.

L130152   Trafalgar Square, 1908. This is arguably the most famous public open space in the world. Sir Robert Peel called it 'one of the finest sites in Europe'. It was created in the 1830s on the site of the King's Mews and a jumble of decrepit buildings known popularly as Bermuda, Caribee, and Porridge Islands, where the poor of London frequented a plethora of cheap cook-shops.

L130161   Trafalgar Square, 1890. Nelson's column was not the first choice of monument to embellish Trafalgar Square - a Colonel Trench had proposed a great pyramid to dwarf St Paul's. The prestigious monument to England's greatest seaman was erected by public subscription to a design by Railton. Of Portland stone, and 145 ft high, it was erected in 1843. The figure of Nelson was carved from three massive stones, the largest of which weighed thirty tons.

L130062   Trafalgar Square, 1900. Four immense bronze lions by Landseer guard the foot of the memorial. The fountains, conceived by Sir Charles Barry, were considered by some Victorians to detract from the overall magnificence of the monument, 'because of the ridiculous insufficiency of their jets of water'.

L130190   Trafalgar Square, 1890. Trafalgar Square, largely because of its huge size and central position, became a popular place for Londoners to gather. On Sunday 13 November 1887, a crowd of twenty thousand was dispersed by the Life Guards and Grenadier Guards with fixed bayonets, after defying a police order against public processions approaching the square on Sunday.

L130218 St Giles Circus, 1910. A bustling street scene at the junction of Oxford Street and the Charing Cross Road. We think of advertising as a modern phenomenon. Yet the Victorian businessman was never slow nor discreet in proclaiming his sales message. These omnibuses are smothered in posters for legendary brands – Dewar's Whisky, Schweppes, Pears Soap, and Swan Vestas.

L130215 St Giles, 1885. It is difficult to tell what these traders are selling, but it is probably wet fish. It looks as if they have almost cleared their tray. A young boy pauses on his way to buy a jug of beer. The commercial streets of the West End were always thronged with street traders pushing their handcarts, who returned at night to slum areas of the East End.

L130142 Westminster Abbey, *c.*1867. This sublime abbey, scene of many coronations down the centuries, is probably the most famous of English religious buildings, and considered the pinnacle of European Gothic. Henry II began the reshaping of Edward the Confessor's old church. Restyling continued until well into the sixteenth century. The abbey was embellished by its lofty twin towers in the early 1700s.

L130150   Westminster Abbey, 1908. Behind are Big Ben and the Houses of Parliament. In the foreground is the Westminster Column, an imposing monument of red granite, designed by Gilbert Scott, in memory of scholars of Westminster School who had fallen in the Crimea. Four imposing lions crouch at its base.

L130188   Houses of Parliament, 1886. This 'superb temple of legislation' in Tudor Gothic was built to replace the old medieval Palace which burned down in 1834. Covering nearly eight acres of ground, it was constructed to Sir Charles Barry's design, although its intricate ornament and detailing were conceived and wrought by that master of Victorian Gothic, Augustus Pugin. The overall cost was £3,000,000.

L130149 Houses of Parliament, 1908. The finest prospect of Barry's Palace of Westminster is to be enjoyed from the river, where the façade extends to a length of almost a 1000 feet. The strong vertical detailing was clearly intended to create the impression of a just and God-fearing Parliament aspiring to the Heavenly virtues.

L130162 Houses of Parliament, 1890. In 1848 a serious drainage problem was discovered inside the Parliament building. A main sewer, passing directly underneath, was discharging into the river under Westminster Bridge. The malodorous gas from this sewer was so dreadful that it extinguished the lamps of the investigating party. Many of the underground apartments were found to be little more than open cesspools.

L130008   Parliament Square, 1890. This monumental clock tower, surmounted by a richly-decorated belfry and spire, is known more popularly as Big Ben, and was designed by E B Denison in 1858 after considerable technical difficulties. The great bell, weighing sixteen tons, was cast at Stockton-on-Tees. It is thought that the clock tower was named after Sir Benjamin Hall, the Commissioner of Works for the project.

L1305068 Lambeth Palace, *c.*1955. On the south bank of the Thames, opposite the Palace of Westminster is this handsome building, for centuries the official residence of the Archbishops of Canterbury. The entrance is through a Gothic gateway, the ground floor of which was once a prison. The Lollard's Tower adjoins the west end of the chapel. Here the Lollards, followers of Wycliffe, were imprisoned and tortured.

L1305043 County Hall, *c.*1955. This colossal building, once home of the controversial Greater London Council, was designed by Ralph Knott and begun in 1912. Though it sits heavily on the Embankment, its broad façades and massed arches in the Piranesi style bring it a monumental dignity.

L130039   Parliament Street, 1908. Here Parliament Street runs into the spacious thoroughfare of Whitehall which rushes onwards to join Trafalgar Square. On the extreme left is the diminutive gabled roof of the Horse Guards. Whitehall is the traditional home of the offices of government and here are the Treasury, the Home Office, the Privy Council and, of course, the entrance to Downing Street.

L130016   Parliament Street and Whitehall, 1880. Serious building work is in progress in this normally sedate street. On the extreme right an area has been cordoned off with barriers, and beyond are the towers of hoists and cranes. Steam funnels into the sky from stationary engines and, in the foreground, a handcart is piled high with bricks. The rush-hour traffic presses a way through as best it can.

L130025 Covent Garden Market, 1900. The cries of traders echo through the expansive square, planned by Inigo Jones. The scene has been described by a contemporary guidebook: 'All night long the rumble of heavy wagons seldom ceases, and before daylight the market is crowded. The very loading of these wagons is a wonder, and the wall-like regularity with which cabbages, cauliflowers and turnips are built up to a height of some twelve feet is nothing short of a miracle'.

L130216 Flower Sellers, Covent Garden, 1877. The flower market was no less frenetic. 'In spring time it is occupied by dealers in spring and bedding flowers, and the pavement is aglow with colour of flower and leaf, and in the early summer hundreds of women and girls are busily occupied in shelling peas'.

L120117 Flower Sellers, Covent Garden, 1877. Flower girls were often orphans, boarding in rooms crowded with other street-sellers. Mayhew reports that they sold violets, wall-flowers, stocks, pinks and roses - anything, in fact, that could be forced and was sweet-smelling. 'Gentlemen are our best customers. Ladies have sometimes said: "A penny, my poor girls, here's three-halfpence for the bunch". Or they have given me the price of two bunches for one.'

L130097 Drury Lane, 1870. This narrow, winding lane close by the Strand is home to the city's biggest and most renowned theatre. In late Victorian times, the modern taste for 'flimsy pieces' made a run at Drury Lane a 'hazardous speculation', because of its huge number of seats. The district was a jumble of cheap lodging houses where the street traders of London scratched an existence.

L130180　Charing Cross, 1890. The cross that gave the area its name was destroyed in 1647. From this point all distances in London are measured. Moreover, a line drawn through it is said to separate the London of pleasure and fashion from that of work and business. The railway station occupies the ground floor of the prestigious company-owned Charing Cross Hotel.

L130033   The Strand, 1890. From early morning until midnight, The Strand is London's busiest street and invariably congested with traffic. It was originally the waterside thoroughfare between the City and Westminster, and it is from this that it derives its name. In earlier days The Strand was a threatening neighbourhood, and many travellers preferred to take a boat rather than pick their way along the ill-paved street and be jostled by pickpockets.

L130005   The Strand, 1890. The Strand stretches from Temple Bar in the east to Trafalgar Square in the west. The beautiful church of St. Clement Danes bestrides its centre, and was erected in 1688 from a design by Wren. The mighty tower was added by Gibbs in 1719. It was said that there was 'somehow a greater lightness and gaiety' here than you would find a few hundred yards further where the city workers toiled 'with their hurried walk and preoccupied look'.

L130191　The Strand, 1915. The Gaiety Theatre dominates the corner where the Aldwych breaks off from the Strand. Theatre goers were enjoying performances by Jose Collins in *Our Nell*. The glittering building was designed by the very fashionable architect Norman Shaw and opened to theatre goers in 1903. It replaced an older theatre of the same name set between Wellington Street and Catherine Street.

L130304　The Aldwych, *c.*1920. Five years on from the previous photograph, the play showing at the Gaiety Theatre is *Love Lies* starring Stanley Lupino. The Aldwych sweeps off sharply to the north towards Kingsway, leaving an island of fine buildings between it and the Strand. The scheme for the development of the locality was completed in 1905, involving the demolition of twenty-eight acres of crooked lanes and ways.

THE CITY

In 1800 the City coughed under a pall of smoke. It was described as 'a hotch potch of half-moon and serpentine narrow streets, close, dismal, long lanes, stinking allies, dark, gloomy courts and suffocating yards'. Here were the homes and businesses of small shopmen, and of the countless craftsmen who laboured in their dark, close workshops.

Once the square mile of the City had been the heart and soul of London. Since the Great Fire city merchants had lived graceful lives in grand houses here. They had powered the creation of Britain's Empire. In the nineteenth century all this was to change as the money industries swelled and the City became financier to the world. Burgeoning institutions and companies demanded and were granted ever greater space. Whole neighbourhoods of the old City were demolished to make way for sham-Gothic office buildings. In 1850 there had been 130,000 residents. By 1900 the figure had sunk to 27,000. The square mile throbbed with industry during the day but was silent and empty at night.

L1305039 The Old Curiosity Shop, *c.*1955. This quaint old house sits on a corner in Lincoln's Inn Fields. It has been claimed, probably erroneously, that it is the original of 'the Old Curiosity Shop' made immortal by Dickens as the home of 'Little Nell'. In this 1950s view it has become an exclusive antique shop but in Victorian times it was a rather dingy emporium owned by H. Poole, jobbing stationer and waste paper merchant.

L130069 Holborn, 1890. This renowned thoroughfare, a continuation of Oxford Street, links the West End with the City. It takes its name from the Oldbourne Bridge which once spanned the Fleet River. At the foot of the picture is a brewer's dray with stretched canvas tilt. Bowler-hatted clerks enjoy some rare refreshing breezes on the upper deck of horse-drawn buses, en route for their daily incarceration in city offices.

L130136   Staple Inn, *c.*1870. Opposite Gray's Inn Road is Staple Inn. It was once the meeting place for wool merchants with a custom house where wool dues were collected. Originally the exclusive province of lawyers,   .
in later years many celebrated figures took rooms in the building, including Dr Johnson, who wrote *Rasselas* here to help defray his mother's funeral expenses.

L130174   Staple Inn, *c.*1890. The magnificent frontage of half-timbered work is the finest in London. Here the plaster rendering shown in the previous photograph has been stripped off revealing a wealth of timbers. The shops have been considerably smartened up. New buildings flank it on both sides, that on the right housing a discount bookshop.

L130141   Temple Bar, 1875. This imposing, ornate gateway once stood where the Strand becomes Fleet Street, and was erected in 1672 to a design by Wren. The effigies portray Stuart monarchs. Beneath its arch Queen Victoria and Albert passed on their way to State services at St Paul's. By the 1860s it was causing considerable traffic congestion and there were heated debates in the press about its future. It was finally removed in 1878 and re-erected at Waltham Cross.

L130080 Fleet Street, 1890. 'The newest fashion newspaper and the oldest-style tavern still jostle each other now as they did a century or more ago.' This bustling street was once the home of the British press. The working day here ran for a full twenty-four hours, with printers and reporters crowding the bars day and night. Crowning the scene in the distance is the glorious dome of St Paul's.

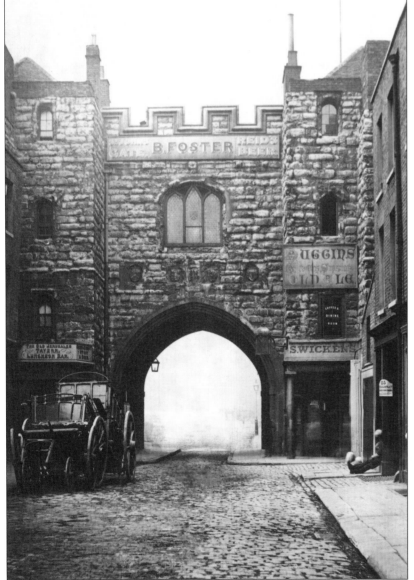

L130144 St John's Gate, Clerkenwell, c.1886. The old gateway to the priory of the Knights of St John stands in St John's Lane, south of the Clerkenwell Road. In the late Gothic style and built with rough-faced stone from a Kent quarry, it was erected by Prior Docwra in 1504. The Old Jerusalem Tavern occupies the ground floor.

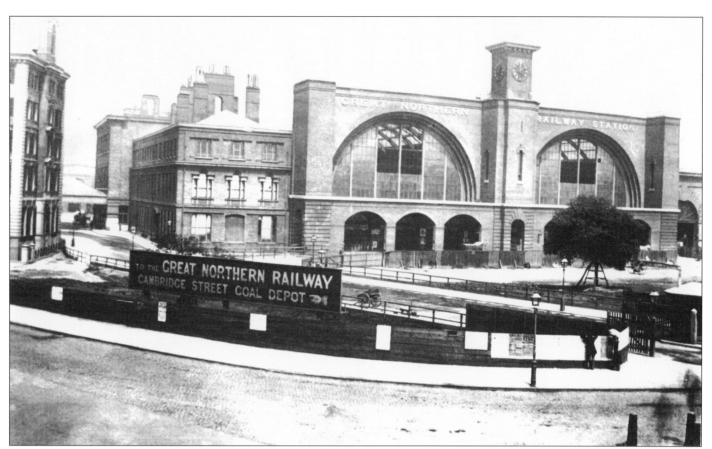

L130067 King's Cross Station, *c.*1886. This London terminus of the Great Northern Railway was opened in 1852. It was built on the site of the old Smallpox Hospital. Its twin brick arches, surmounted by a central clock tower, make it a curiously modern-looking building. There was a granary here that would accept 60,000 sacks of corn, water-tanks holding 150,000 gallons and a goods shed 600 ft long. From King's Cross trains plied the east coast route to Scotland.

L130096 Peter's Lane, Clerkenwell Road, 1880. Close by St John's Gate is this narrow alley of tall tile-hung shops and houses, which lean precariously over, so that residents might almost stretch out and shake hands from their windows. Clerkenwell was the neighbourhood where the jewellers, watchmakers and silversmiths of the City had their workshops. It is said there was always the stench of seal oil, used to lubricate clocks and watches.

L130037   Ludgate Hill, 1897. A locomotive of the L. C. & D Railway has just left Holborn Viaduct Station and thunders south over the bridge, steam ballooning out over the roofs. Below, traffic crawls miserably up Ludgate Hill. In wet weather horses with heavy wagons slipped and slid up to St Paul's. The quagmire became so impassable that a new wooden roadway had to be added.

L130168 New Bridge Street and Queen Victoria Street, 1904. The Hand-in-Hand Fire and Life Insurance Society building stands at the junction of these two streets close by Blackfriars Bridge. It was established in 1696 and by 1890 had amassed accumulated funds of over two million pounds. To its right is the railway bridge from Holborn Viaduct Station.

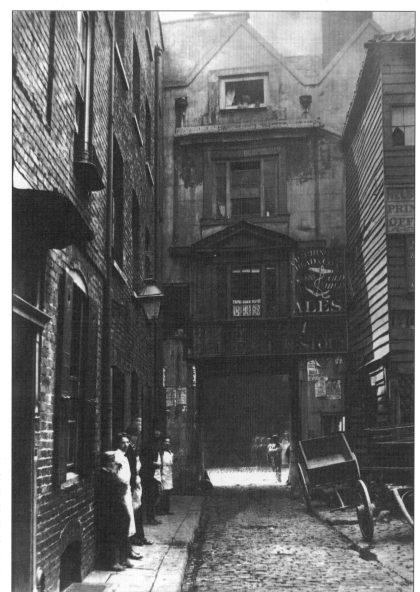

L130122 Oxford Arms, Warwick Lane, c. 1875. This old inn has been serving clients since 1673, and was once an important coaching stop. In the 1860s, after the demise of the stages, many of its rooms were let out to lodgers. However, it was still a strategic terminus for carriers plying between London, Oxford and other regional towns. It finally shut its doors in 1875 and was demolished.

L130126　St Paul's from Across the River, 1890. This panoramic vista of the City and St Paul's was probably taken from the southern tip of Southwark Bridge. In early days Queenhithe on the north bank of the Thames was a significant port for the landing of fish and corn. Its position above London Bridge - the successful docks were all in broader reaches down-river - led to its inevitable decline.

L130078 St Paul's Cathedral, 1890. Perched on the summit of Ludgate Hill at almost the highest point in the City, Wren's masterpiece is the pride of London. In the form of a cross, it is built in the Corinthian style, and surmounted by the giant dome which rises on arches over the centre. Many great men and women are buried here, including Wren himself, James Barry, Sir Joshua Reynolds, Opie and Landseer.

L130164 St Paul's from Cannon Street, 1905. The magnificent elevations of St Paul's soar above the surrounding streets. Wren directed its construction at such a ponderous pace that Parliament cut his salary from £200 to £100 a year. It was not until 1711, when the work was finally completed, that he was repaid the balance owing. In the street the modest cart of the 'People's Caterers' is offering 'machine-made bread'. At the time mechanisation was the way to the future and constituted a distinct trading advantage.

L130055   Queen Victoria Street, 1897. The heart of the Square Mile. City life looks as frenetic as it does today. Job mobility was unheard of in the Victorian office. Only by staying with the same employer was there any hope of security and a modest pension. The best positions were with banks and insurance offices. Those keen to climb the career ladder avoided Law Chambers, which paid the meanest salaries.

L130066   Cheapside, c.1886. In the 1850s, Cheapside was one of the most fashionable shopping streets in London, with a 'mighty stream of traffic' flowing through from Oxford Street to Leadenhall and the City. Because of its prestigious reputation and close proximity to the Bank, city financiers clamoured to live here, and annual rents from a single house could reach the incredible sum of three hundred pounds.

L130273   Cheapside, *c.*1905. At the junction with Paternoster Row, Cheapside swings from the north in an arc and heads east towards the Bank. Paternoster Row, on the right, was once a fashionable shopping street patronised by Pepys and his wife. Nicholson, the haberdasher and milliner on the corner, has an impressive new frontage constructed in 1900. Upstairs are the windows of the workshops and below an exuberant display of hats and laces.

L130177   Mansion House and Cheapside, *c.*1890. In the distance, the graceful Portland stone spire of St Mary le Bow soars sublimely over the City. It was the most expensive of Wren's refurbishments, costing £15,400. The ponderous Victorian Gothic architecture of this part of the City is not to everyone's taste today. Mappin and Webb's corner premises, together with the section of Queen Victoria Street down to Cannon Street, were completed in 1869.

L130209. Mansion House and Cheapside, 1890. Mansion House, the lavish building on the left, has been the official residence of the Lord Mayor for two centuries. It was built by George Dance on the site of the old stocks market. It has been said to have the air of a Roman palazzo. The portico is reached by flights of stone steps from the pavement and, from under the fluted columns, city workers could watch the throng of traffic passing below.

L130192   Mansion House and Cheapside, 1915. The foundation stone of the Mansion House was laid in 1739. The façade is so hemmed in by the street and the buildings opposite, that it could never achieve the visual impact its architects would have wished for. The buses chugging along below are still open-topped. It would be another ten years before roofs were added to the London General Omnibus Company's fleets.

L130208   The Bank of England and the Royal Exchange, 1890. In front of the Royal Exchange the wide pavement reaches out like a promontory. Richard Jefferies described the scene in the 1880s: 'Like the spokes of a wheel converging, streams of human life flow into this agitated pool. . . Blue carts and yellow omnibuses, varnished carriages and brown vans, pale loads of yellow straw, rusty-red iron clanking on paintless carts, high white wool-packs. . .sunlight sparkling on brass harness. . .this is the vortex and whirlpool, the centre of human life today on the earth'.

L130179   The Bank of England, 1890. Opposite the Mansion House is the Bank of England, a single-storey monolithic edifice, designed in 1734 by George Sampson. Sir John Soane devised some alterations to the west elevation in 1788. In late Victorian times there were nine hundred employees with salaries ranging from £50 to £1,200. The total salary bill was £210,000 - the sum a single top manager might earn today!

L130181   The Bank of England and the Royal Exchange, 1886. In 1838 there was a great conflagration which began in the rooms of Lloyd's coffee-house. Thousands of tons of masonry fell and the old Royal Exchange was destroyed. The new Exchange was designed by William Tite and built at a furious pace. Within three years it was open for business. A mass of buildings was cleared from in front and Chantrey's equestrian statue of the Duke of Wellington erected in the broad space that had been created.

L130153   The Bank of England and the Royal Exchange, 1908. In the late nineteenth century a commentator pointed out that 'the stranger will be particularly struck with the absence of women from the moving crowd in Cheapside, and indeed generally in the City'. This was to change very soon: young women would soon be taking over the office desks as typing-pools were established - the first typewriter appeared in the 1880s.

L130207   The Bank of England and the Royal Exchange, *c.*1910. In the 1860s the economist Bagehot described Lombard Street, that runs to the right of the Mansion House, as 'by far the greatest combination of economical power and economic delicacy that the world has ever seen'. With the coming of the railways and international currency dealings, the City began to prosper as it never had before, with small investors flocking to involve themselves in the heady world of stocks and shares.

L130012   The Royal Exchange, 1886. The frieze that tops the Corinthian portico proclaims in Latin that the Exchange was founded in the thirteenth year of Queen Elizabeth, and restored in the seventh of Queen Victoria. The pediment above features figures sculpted by Richard Westmacott, representing Commerce holding the charter of the Exchange, attended by the Lord Mayor and merchants.

L130193   Threadneedle Street and the Royal Exchange, *c.*1910. Omnibuses advertising Dunlop tyres enter Threadneedle Street. Here was the famous American Coffee House, where merchants with interests in the colonies met to discuss business. On the right is a horse-drawn cart of the Royal Mail.

L130102   King William Street, 1880. This photograph shows the Cannon Street end of King William Street, which heads south-east from the Mansion House towards London Bridge. This dignified thoroughfare was conceived in 1835, and was much admired for its spacious and airy atmosphere. On the left is the City Luncheon Bar, and in the foreground a fleet of carrier's carts owned by Henry Drapper.

L130187 The Monument, *c*.1890. At the foot of King William Street is Wren's mighty fluted Doric column of Portland stone, erected to commemorate the Great Fire of London in 1666. It was one of the tourist attractions of the City to climb to the top, and in 1842 rails were added to the lofty gallery to prevent suicides. In *Martin Chuzzlewit* the keeper considered it 'quite worth twice the money not to make the ascent'.

L130018   London Bridge, 1890. In the background is the Monument, rising over the roofs of Adelaide House, home of the Pearl Assurance Company. This squat building was demolished in 1920, and underneath was found one of the arches of the old London Bridge. London Bridge would seem to have been closed off to traffic. There are flags flying so possibly the crowds have come to enjoy a civic procession.

L130131   The King's Head, Borough High Street, 1875. This old inn, just over the river from London Bridge, was called by Stow 'one of the fair inns' of Southwark. In 1720 it was described as 'well built, handsome, and enjoying a good trade'. In this view it looks a ramshackle establishment, with Chinese-style latticed balconies and shabby cellars. It had shut up shop by 1885.

L130251　The Tower Of London, *c*.1920. This stunning panorama looks south-east over the battlements and roofs of London's most celebrated building and towards the river and Tower Bridge. The pinnacles of the White Tower pierce the city sky.

L1305022 The Tower of London, *c*.1955. Tugs towing flat-bottomed barges are still plying the Thames in this 1950s scene. Seventy years before there was a timber quay under the walls of the Tower, with tall-masted sailing ships edging through the raised bascules of Tower Bridge. The river here was thick with islands of logs chained together, floating heavily in the shallows.

L130172   The Tower of London, *c*.1890. This ancient fortress has served as arsenal, prison and royal residence, and is comprised of an irregular mass of buildings erected at various periods down the centuries. It was begun by William The Conqueror, and it is his keep, the White Tower, that still dominates the scene. The moat was drained in 1843 and sown with grasses and shrubs.

L130071   The Tower of London, 1890.   The Tower has four entrances: the Iron Gate, the Water Gate, and the Traitor's Gate – all facing the River Thames. Traitor's Gate was the entrance used by many illustrious and infamous figures on their way to execution, including Sir Thomas More, Anne Boleyn, Katherine Howard and the Earl of Essex.

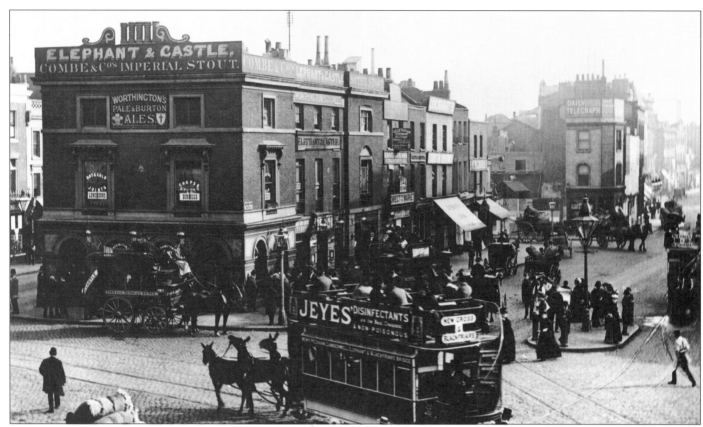

L130028   The Elephant and Castle, *c.*1890.This crowded region south of the river was once the heart of London cockney life. The Elephant and Castle, a great meeting place of thoroughfares, was termed a 'ganglion of roads' by Dickens in *Bleak House*. The squat old inn that gave it its name dominates the scene, and is offering hot and cold joints, chops and steaks to diners. In the foreground a porter hauls a weighty load of sacks on a simple two-wheeled handcart.

L130029   The Bull and Bush, North End Road, 1899. Close by Hampstead Heath, in the leafy northern fringes of Victorian London, is this picturesque old inn, which was once the haunt of the writer Addison and his friends. With its terrace and gardens, private dining rooms, coffee house and billiard rooms, it offered hospitality to the intellectual and bohemian classes of Georgian London. Note the rustic wooden arch over the porch on the right.

L130147, Crystal Palace, 1900. This monumental glass pleasure dome was created in Hyde Park by Joseph Paxton for the Great Exhibition of 1851. Two thousand workers erected it at high speed, bolting and welding together 3,300 iron columns, 205 miles of sash-bars and 293,655 panes of glass! It was a temple to the triumphs of Victorian art and industry. After the Exhibition, it was moved to wooded parkland at Sydenham in south-east London.

L130059 Crystal Palace, c.1890. Pleasure seekers make the most of the winter weather skating on one of the many lakes. The Crystal Palace became a paradise for Londoners keen to escape the dirt and the grime. At weekends they flocked to Sydenham in their thousands to enjoy the displays and exhibitions - Blondin once walked a high wire here and cooked an omelette seventy ft in the air!

L130060   Crystal Palace, 1890. This ornate pleasure craft looks perilously low in the water, but the throng of passengers seem quite oblivious of the rising water levels. Queen Victoria was a regular visitor to the Crystal Palace, and once encouraged the Shah of Persia to sample its delights. These pleasure grounds were an unparalleled symbol of the continuing glories and achievements of her reign.

L130210   A Tavern Scene, 1885. The public house has long been a vital constituent of city life. Here customers could relax after the day's toil with a tankard of porter. In the Victorian era the tavern became the exclusive haunt of the poor. The coming of the notorious gin-houses, combined with Victorian prudery and fears of vice, encouraged the more well-to-do to frequent safer restaurants and hotels. As Dickens pointed out: 'Gin drinking is a great vice in England'. The simple pleasure of a pot and a pipe were largely ousted.

THE DIAMOND JUBILEE

Queen Victoria lived from 1819 to 1901. Her reign spanned two generations. By 1850 her loyal subjects had borrowed their sovereigns name and were calling themselves 'Victorians'. The young and popular Queen reigned over a land that ruled the world, and her subjects were proud of her and of their country's achievements and potential. Britain was in the midst of creating the world's first great industrial power and it necessarily involved a process of upheaval and social change.

Inherent was a deep-ingrained instinct for nationalism which bonded the nation together in difficult and troublesome times. The Victorians were never slow in celebrating a civic occasion, and thronged the streets whenever a gesture of loyalty to queen and country was required. It is not surprising, therefore, that when the time of her Diamond Jubilee came around that the whole of London flocked to honour her. They cheered the military and its colourful pageantry, the endless procession of carriages containing dignitaries and, most of all, their beloved queen. *Vanity Fair* pronounced on the day's proceedings: 'We are a great people and we realised it on Saturday as we never realised it before'.

L130157   Buckingham Palace, 1897. The royal coach heads out across the courtyard of the Palace bound for The Mall. A throng of carriages waits to join the procession across London. Queen Victoria wrote in her diary that it was 'a never-to-be-forgotten day. . . No one ever, I believe, has met with such an ovation as was given to me . . . Every face seemed to be filled with real joy'.

L130011   The Albert Memorial, 1897. Crowds gather on the steps of Gilbert Scott's imposing Gothic-inspired memorial to the Queen's beloved husband, Albert. The Guards' bandsmen, resplendent in busbies and bright red uniforms, are waiting to begin their procession. Their sonorous music was sure to stir her subjects to overwhelming declarations of loyalty and patriotism.

L130158   Diamond Jubilee Day, 1897. Queen Victoria smiles graciously at her subjects from beneath a parasol. The team of horses bend under the weight of shining brasses and decorative tackle. Behind the coach stand a gathering of be-robed dignitaries of the Church.

L130219   Westminster Bridge, 1897. Jubilee day was the perfect occasion for royal pageantry. After a service at St Paul's, the ageing Queen was driven in her state coach past Parliament and across this crowded bridge, escorted by her loyal troops. The bridge is decked with garlands.

STREET CHARACTERS

The streets of London were thick with beggars and confidence tricksters. A guidebook in 1888 suggested the following action be taken by travellers if they were accosted: 'To get rid of your beggar, when wearisome, take no notice of him at all. He will follow you till you meet a more likely person, but no farther'. Yet many beggars were making desperate efforts to lift themselves and their families out of unrelenting poverty by taking on a trade, however small and insignificant. The match sellers, shoe blacks and flower girls, many displaced from the countryside where life was yet more unendurable, were given short shrift by many of the great and wealthy. The same guide suggests: 'If your tormentor has anything to sell, reply simply, "Got one," and pass on.'

Street traders faced suspicion from the public and persecution by the police on a daily basis. Their lives were a continual struggle to win food and shelter. Many lived in cheap, overcrowded lodging houses in poor areas of the West End and the City, where they were preyed upon by voracious landlords. There was, of course, no social relief, and families were forced back to their own cunning and guile to keep body and soul together.

L130116   The Match Seller, 1884. Selling a few lucifer's was all too often the pretext for begging. Bryant and May employed seven hundred girls to sell their matches on the streets. In 1888 these girls went on strike for better pay and conditions. Such a protest and threat to public order was rare amongst itinerant workers.

L130111 Ginger Cake Seller, 1884. This dark-coloured cake of flour, treacle and ground ginger was a favourite snack with Victorians at fairs and street events. The roughly-shaped pieces were measured into paper cones. This old man's gingercake was probably made by his wife or daughters.

L130114   The Shoeblack, 1895. The bootblack business grew into a highly-organised and philanthropic affair. Sporting their red uniforms, the bootblack boys were a familiar sight on the streets of London. The Ragged Schools, Saffron Hill, set up the first society, and nine others followed. The aim was to educate orphan boys and to give them a good start in the world.

L130119 Shoeblacks, c.1890. By the 1880s the shoeblack societies had four hundred boys on their books. A number of them were given cheap board and lodging. These shoeblacks were licensed to trade by the Metropolitan Police and carried on their business unhindered. There were, however, many unofficial operators, subject to no discipline or supervision, who 'infested the streets and annoyed the passenger'.

L1302002 The Water Seller, c.1890. There were continual public fears about the purity of London's water supply. In early Victorian times water taken from the Thames at Chelsea was infected with the contents of the city's sewers and the drainings from its dunghills. There were terrible widespread cholera outbreaks in the 1840s and 50s. The water seller shown here would have had a regular pitch so that clients grew to trust the purity of his water.

L130108   The Dancing Bear, 1895. Bears had long been abused by Londoners. In the seventeenth century there was a popular bear garden at Bankside. This poor creature is urged to dance to bugle tunes played by his owner, who is probably an old soldier. Though tightly muzzled, this giant seven-foot bear must have terrified passers-by, as he bayed and complained at his miserable lot.

L1302004 The Newspaper Seller, c.1890. A bewildering number of morning and evening newspapers was available to the Victorian reading public, including the *Daily Chronicle, The Times, The Evening News* and the *Morning Advertiser*. In the 1880s and 90s, new printing technology released onto the market a wide range of cheap and tacky weekly magazines and comics. This old newspaper woman stands her ground under the spinning wheels of passing carriages.

L1302001 The Potato Seller, *c.*1890. This street trading woman is offering potatoes from her basket. Baked potatoes were even more popular with Londoners, and handcarts fitted with ovens and chimneys plied the streets offering inexpensive hot snacks. She looks relaxed enough but the weight of the potatoes must be excruciating.

L130109   The Organ Grinder, 1895. The barrel organ always drew a huge crowd with its wheezy renderings of popular tunes. When a trio of frightened monkeys was introduced, the attraction for children was irresistible. Here they crowd closely round while the monkeys, dressed in waistcoats are goaded reluctantly into performing their tricks.

L130115 The Chimney Sweep, 1884. Mayhew reports that sweepers were a tight-knit community. Master sweepers often let room to families in the same trade. The climbing boys, often from the Workhouse, earned 2*d* or 3*d* a day, but were sometimes given an extra 6*d* by grateful householders. They climbed easily up through wide flues using their elbows and legs, but often got stuck or nearly suffocated in narrow nine-inch chimneys. For young children it must have been a terrifying experience.

L130110   Hokey Pokey Stall, Greenwich, 1884. Children cluster round licking at the cheap ice cream from the hokey pokey stall. They look like ragged street urchins in their rumpled suits and battered boots, and were probably bought their treats in return for posing for the photographer.

L130167   The Cutler, 1890. The late Victorian era was one of immense change. Machines had taken over the production of many household gadgets that had been previously made by individual craftsmen. This mechanisation caused terrible unemployment. Many older tradesmen, unable to find work, took to the streets with their handcarts.

L130214   The Knife Sharpener, Whitechapel Road, 1885. This cutler and locksmith has an established stall in the market in the Whitechapel Road. He is a general jobber, able to sharpen knives and tools, re-set saws, repair locks and cut replacement keys. Hanging on the rail behind are huge clumps of keys.

L130212 Nomads, 1885. Vagrants have wandered the fields and lanes of Britain down the centuries. Subject to no laws they were the truly free people of the world. The Vagrancy Act of 1824 made it illegal for them to be out in the open air without visible means of subsistence. Life became suddenly more complicated. The Reading-style caravan in the photograph was a new introduction. Families followed the country fairs and markets and often ventured into London for the festivals and fairs held on the commons.

L130112   The Chair Mender, 1877. There were once 2,500 cabinet-making shops in London, many employing children. When steam-powered sawmills and mechanical production methods introduced ready-made furniture onto the market, thousands of craftsmen lost their jobs. Here, an old man re-canes a child's chair. The housekeeper maintains a wary eye on his progress.

L130213   The Strawberry Seller, 1885. This rather forlorn picture shows a tiny emaciated pony pulling a cart selling strawberries. We associate this exotic and scarce fruit with jollity and celebration, but this trader and her son radiate only a sense of misery and poverty.

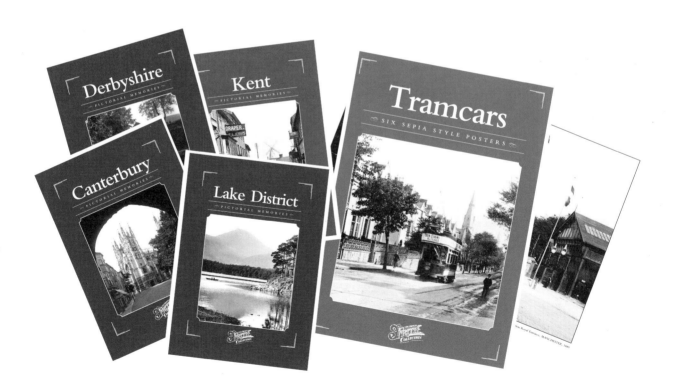

Themed Poster Books £4.99

000-7	Canals and Waterways	
001-5	High Days and Holidays	
003-1	Lakes and Rivers	
004-x	Piers	
005-8	Railways	
044-9	Ships	
002-3	Stone Circles & Ancient Monuments	
007-4	Tramcars	

Town & City Series £9.99

010-4	Brighton & Hove	
015-5	Canterbury	
012-0	Glasgow & Clydeside	
011-2	Manchester	
040-6	York	

Town & City series Poster Books £5.99

018-x	Around Brighton	
023-6	Canterbury	
043-0	Derby	
020-1	Glasgow	
011-2	Manchester	
041-4	York	

County Series £9.99

024-4	Derbyshire	
028-7	Kent	
029-5	Lake District	
031-7	Leicestershire	
026-0	London	
027-9	Norfolk	
030-9	Sussex	
025-2	Yorkshire	

County Series Poster Books £4.99

032-5	Derbyshire	
036-8	Kent	
037-6	Lake District	
039-2	Leicestershire	
034-1	London	
035-x	Norfolk	
038-4	Sussex	
033-3	Yorkshire	

Available
soon

County Series £9.99

045-7	Berkshire	
053-8	Buckinghamshire	
055-4	East Anglia	
077-5	Greater London	
051-1	Lancashire	
047-3	Staffordshire	
049-x	Warwickshire	
063-5	West Yorkshire	

County Series Poster Books £4.99

046-5	Berkshire	
054-6	Buckinghamshire	
056-2	East Anglia	
078-3	Greater London	
052-x	Lancashire	
048-1	Staffordshire	
050-3	Warwickshire	
064-3	West Yorkshire	

Country Series £9.99

075-9	Ireland	
071-6	North Wales	
069-4	South Wales	
073-2	Scotland	

Country Series Poster Books £4.99

076-7	Ireland	
072-4	North Wales	
070-8	South Wales	
074-0	Scotland	

A selection of our 1999 programme:
County Series and Poster Books
Devon, Cornwall, Essex,
Nottinghamshire, Cheshire.

Town and City Series and Poster Books
Bradford, Edinburgh, Liverpool, Nottingham,
Stamford, Bristol, Dublin,
Stratford-upon-Avon, Bath, Lincoln,
Cambridge, Oxford, Matlock, Norwich.

Themed Poster Books
Castles, Fishing, Cricket, Bridges, Cinemas,
The Military, Cars.